SNORP'S ADVENTURE

MARKOSIA

THOMAS ROGERS - AARON MORAN

SAMANTHA READER
EDITOR

FOR **MARKOSIA ENTERPRISES** LTD

HARRY MARKOS
PUBLISHER & MANAGING PARTNER

GM JORDAN
SPECIAL PROJECTS CO-ORDINATOR

ANNIKA EADE
MEDIA MANAGER

ANDY BRIGGS
CREATIVE CONSULTANT

MEIRION JONES
MARKETING DIRECTOR

IAN SHARMAN
EDITOR IN CHIEF

ISBN 978-1-913359-30-0

www.markosia.com

On the edge of the galaxy, there is a planet called Glum. It is home to the Snorps and has a magical lighthouse that gives light to the planet.

One day, the lighthouse broke in a magical storm scattering magical star pieces across the planet. The Snorps knew that, if this ever happened, it was their job to fix it.

Each of the Snorp tribes met and talked about how to solve the problem. The Snorp tribes would find each of the star orbs and return them to the lighthouse.

If the lighthouse wasn't turned back on the planet would be lost in darkness and the Shadow Witches would return with their evil minions, the Glorps. Each tribe set off across the planet of Glum in search of the lost star orbs.

One of the Snorp Tribe set off to the Gloom Shroom Forest, where one of the star pieces was seen to have fallen. It was here the star piece was found.

One by one the Snorps left the forest, when suddenly trouble struck. With a large crack the bridge collapsed and the Purple Snorp holding the star orb was washed away.

Purple awoke and standing above him was a glowing mushroom. "Hello my name is Gloom; you look lost." Purple knew he needed help and explained to the Gloom Shroom the trouble they were all in.

"So, you're telling me if we don't fix the lighthouse everything will go dark? We best get a move on then," and so Purple Snorp and the Gloom Shroom became friends, setting off on their adventure.

Purple and Gloom walked around the dark forest trying to find their way out. Gloom told him the story of the sleeping forest and why it was so dark. It was Gloom Shroom's job to make sure the bulbs were working properly but the Eyecrids had eaten the trees bulbs.

Purple could see the sadness in Gloom and wondered if there was a way to fix the problem.

The Snorp had an idea and used the magical power of the star orb. Suddenly the forest burst into life and lights in the trees began to sparkle. Then one of the trees started to speak, "What is that light that you hold, furry creature?"

Purple told him the story and where he needed to go. He explained that the Eyecrids had only eaten the tree's bulbs because they wanted to sleep.

The forest had found peace once again. Purple explained that a little misunderstanding created so much trouble and they could all be friends.

After bringing peace to the forest the Snorp and Gloom were pointed in the direction of the Icesheet Mountains to seek the help of the Yetis.

When walking along the rocky path the pair came across a robot lying by a large rock.

Purple tapped the robot with the star orb and the robot awoke.

"Thanks, my battery had run out! My name is X7 and I'm an explorer robot."

X7 joined the two friends. They climbed the mountains, overcoming the ice boulders that fell towards them by blasting them with X7's laser eyes.

Across the ice swept mountains they travelled, following the path the forest had told them, on the back of their large metal friend until they came across a large ice field.

At first it seemed empty until X7 observed large shapes in the distance. They had reached the Yeti's playground.

Purple asked for the Yeti king's help and told the Yetis his story.

"Of course, we will help. My brave daughter will join you on this quest!"

The Yeti king invited Purple Snorp and his friends to stay in the great hall and enjoy the Snow Ball. Gloom cheered at the idea of a warm fire!

Purple was sitting by the fire at the party when he heard a female voice, "Hi, I'm Gummbella but my friends call me Bella, my father told me I am to guide you through the mountains."

Bella told the Snorp about the caverns of lava they would have to go through.

An old yeti appeared before them and started to speak. "I must warn you," he said, "of a fire Genie from the faraway land of Volcania, who was tricked into creating the tallest of mountains."

"But in doing so he became trapped. The mountains he created are the ones you see today"

He handed the Snorp a bottle of freezing air and told him to use it when the time came. Purple drifted off to sleep and dreamt of finally getting home.

The next day they crossed the mountains until they reached a large cave that took them deep into the earth. Gloom's light helped them to see in the cavern's darkness.

Finally, they reached a great lake of lava. Purple opened the bottle of air, freezing the lava.

The cave echoed with a mighty roar as a sleeping fire
Genie awoke. "Who dares disturb my slumber?"

"Everyone jump on," said X7. They jumped onto the robot's
back. Trapped and with the ice melting, X7's hands turned
into propellers.

The robot held them up and suddenly the group was
surfing the waves of lava crashing through the cave's exit
and tumbled down the mountain side.

The group fell down into the Slip Slop Swamp. Sinking into the muddy waters, a strange eye creature that looked like a snail saved them.

The large snail acted as a boat, slowly taking the group on a tour of the swamps. Mystical lights danced in the distance as bird creatures with round heads watched from the branches.

Bella was looking around the swamp with suspicion, "Father said that a witch lives in these swamps, a witch that curses anyone who stands in her way." X7 stood like the silent protector of the group.

"I see land," X7 pointed as suddenly from out of the mist a small island revealed itself, on it sat a house and green smoke spilled from the chimney.

The group landed on the island where a lady in black was waiting on the shore.

"Welcome, come into my home," said the lady and led them into the hut, Purple felt uneasy.

"So, lost Snorp, how can I, the witch of the swamp, help you? I see you are carrying a piece of the fallen star."

The Snorp was concerned about the witch's behaviour towards the starlight. Purple explained what had happened and where they were heading. "I see, I see, come over to the cauldron." Snorp and the others followed the witch.

"I can help you on your way but first you must hand over the star orb," the witch began to cackle. Purple turned and started to leave, worried about the witch taking the piece.

"Now you are here, little Snorp, I can't let you go; it was I that broke the lighthouse."

Suddenly Glorps appeared from everywhere; a trap had been sprung. Behind each bookcase waited at least ten Glorps holding sharp spears.

The group was surrounded, and the circle was closing in fast. The witch started to speak, but this time in a more sinister voice. "Let me introduce myself. I am Agnaa queen of the Shadow Witches."

"It appears we are in a jam," said X7. Gloom started to panic as the Glorps' spears came closer. Bella pointed at a hole in the roof of the cottage. In an instant X7's right arm extended for the others to run up

Bella used her strength to push the cauldron over; magical missiles exploded everywhere as they made their escape onto the roof before sliding down the outside, landing in the soft mud of the swamp island before making a break for freedom.

They continued for a couple of hours until they reached the edge of a cliff, from which the swamp's water spilled over. "Wow, look at that, it's an ocean of cloud," said Bella. The clouds tumbled over each other like waves on the ocean.

The group looked across the vast sea of cloud. "How will we cross?" replied Gloom, his light dimmed at the thought. Purple noticed what looked like a giant horn sitting there on the edge of the cliff

Purple walked up and blew into it.

Bursting from the clouds a city appeared on the back of a giant octopus.

The tentacle landed on the edge of the cliff, a road was paved along the tentacle and tall thin figures marched along it. They looked like grasshoppers dressed in armour, the one at the front was wearing a top hat and very bizarre orange trousers.

The tall figure started to speak, "Hello I am the Royal Ambassador of her Highness of the Dingle Dangle nation; we welcome you to Octopolis. We know all about your situation, let me escort you to the palace."

Purple and his fellow companions entered the great palace, its courtyard was filled with many fountains spurting water high into the air.

They passed through a large set of red oak doors into the main throne room. They walked down the red carpet and saw great waterfalls pouring from the walls. When they reached the throne, they were greeted by the Queen of the Dingle Dangles.

"Brave Snorp, I have heard of your journey towards the great lighthouse, the time of darkness is near and I am afraid I have upsetting news."

The Queen explained how the other Snorp tribe's star pieces had been stolen, without them the Ever Night would be upon them.

"Fear not, brave Snorp, for I have a gift for you," she clapped her hands and the door to the right opened. Bounding out of the door came a great four-legged creature with scales and what almost looked like a beard. Flames burst from the creature's mouth and nose as it barked into the air.

"This is a Dragonboon, they are great at finding things and I feel he will be of great help, he is called Snark."

Tonight, we shall enjoy the festival of light. Join me on the highest tower," said the Queen.

Purple Snorp watched the festival of light feeling hopeful that he could save his friends and loved ones.

The next day when the group met up outside the palace her highness was waiting on a large floating ship docked just outside the palace gates. Gloom looked in awe at the amount of airships that whizzed around in the sea of clouds.

They walked onto the deck where the Queen was waiting, "We must launch our operation immediately; time is of the essence. We will draw the Glorps' attention while you sneak in and get the star pieces that have been stolen."

They travelled for days across the clouds until they saw a purple glow in the distance, the ships went below the clouds. Purple looked over the side of the ship to find pure darkness swirling like a whirlpool constantly moving like an inky black ocean.

At the centre of the blackness sat a large fortress made of iron. The ambassador approached the Queen. "Your highness we are approaching the Glorp fort, what are your orders?"

The Queen hesitated; she looked at the group and smiled. "We shall give them a chance and let the Glorps know we are here"

She held up her staff and released a pink flare into the air. Suddenly balls of fire came from the fort towards the ships. "We will draw their attention, now go."

X7 picked everyone up, putting them on his back before jumping off the ship. His arms turned into wings and they glided down towards the fortress.

As they started to land, X7's feet turned into drills, crashing into the castle and cutting through its many floors.

The group crashed down amongst the Glorps and Purple could see the stolen star pieces in a glass orb next to Agnaa. Hanging from the ceiling above them was a cage that imprisoned a group of Snorps from other tribes including a very sad looking pink Snorp. Agnaa stood from her throne. "Get them," she screeched, lightning coming from her hands.

X7 dashed in front of Snorp and put up a barrier protecting them from Agnaa's powers. "Purple, get the star pieces, we will distract them," shouted Gumbella as she picked Snark up by his tail and began spinning with him as flames burst from the Dragonboon's mouth, sending Glorps fleeing.

Purple and Gloom danced between the Glorps' spears, X7 fired a laser from his eyes sending the cage with the trapped Snorps plummeting to the ground, breaking the door.

The pink Snorp grabbed the star pieces and ran towards Gloom as Snorp signalled X7 to get them out of there.

They landed back on the Queen's ship. "Cast off!" shouted the Queen.

The Dingle Dangle ships followed her majesty's vessel through the black storm clouds of the shadow plains, lighting crackled as the Glorp ships chased them through the clouds..

They ducked in and out like a big game of cat and mouse. X7 fired his lasers at any incoming cannonballs while Gummbella commanded the deck. Gloom stood at the front of the ship lighting the way.

Snorp knew how to make the ship go faster. He gathered all the Snorps, including Snark, at the back of the ship. The Snorps rubbed themselves against Snark's belly and flames blew from Snark. The tickling created bigger and bigger flames, sending the ship flying forwards in a burst of speed.

The ship burst from the magical storm into a sea of blue sky.

"Look Sanctum!" shouted Gloom. They could see the lighthouse but something was wrong, a cloud of darkness swirled above the lighthouse. "We are too late," said Pink Snorp.

Let's not lose hope yet, there is always a way to fix things" replied Bella. The ship circled the top of the tower, the Glorp ships had closed in on them.

"Don't they ever give up?" said Gloom. "How are we going to land?"

"I don't have enough energy to fly, but I'm certain I can make a short jump," X7 answered. With that, X7 gathered up all his friends. He sprinted towards the edge of the ship and leapt; Gloom passed out in fear that they could miss.

They hurtled towards a balcony around the middle of lighthouse.

"We are going too fast," shouted Gumbella. Gloom was still unconscious, but Snark enjoyed the wind in his slobbery face.

As they came into land X7 activated the thrusters on the bottom of his feet, slowing their fall. Gloom awoke with a shriek as they touched down safely on top of the lighthouse.

Purple Snorp put the star orbs into the glass machine.

As the machine started to power up there was a sudden cackle, Agnaa the Shadow Witch had appeared, floating around the top of the lighthouse.

"You are too late" she said, as lightning bounced towards the Snorps.

"It seems she doesn't give up" said X7. "Quickly, Purple, activate the machine!"

Purple Snorp darted towards the lever on the machine, but it was just out of reach; the star piece was now floating in the glass case of the machine, waiting to be released.

"Quick, to me," said Purple Snorp. As Pink ran towards him the Snorp linked his fingers to give her a leg up. Her foot touched his hands and he flung Pink towards the lever.

The Snorp landed on the lever, pulling it down with her weight, the machine started to rumble sending a bright green ray of light straight into the portal of darkness that loomed overhead. There was a rumble followed by an explosion of light as the portal folded in on itself.

Agnaa let out a cry as the light from the explosion engulfed her. The Ever Night had been stopped just in time and Agnaa the Shadow Witch was nowhere to be seen. Snorp and his companions had saved the day.

With Agnaa's magic gone, the Glorps turned back into the friendly Snorps! Everyone rejoiced as light was returned to the world.

Later that evening a giant party took place around the lighthouse with friends from the many lands they had travelled through. Purple and his friends looked up at the stars and realised their adventure had only just begun.

www.ingramcontent.com/pod-product-compliance
Lightning Source LLC
Chambersburg PA
CBHW060857090426
42737CB00023B/3479